Yellow Umbrella Books are published by Capstone Press
151 Good Counsel Drive, P.O. Box 669, Mankato, Minnesota 56002
http://www.capstone-press.com

Library of Congress Cataloging-in-Publication Data
Weidenman, Lauren.
    People and places/by Lauren Weidenman; consulting editor, Gail Saunders-Smith.
    p. cm.
    Includes index.
    ISBN 0-7368-0743-8
    1. Human geography—Juvenile literature. [1. Human geography.] I. Saunders-Smith, Gail.
II. Title.
GF48.W45   2001
304.2—dc21   00-036471

    Summary: Describes the places where people live, including a variety of climates and
    land features.

Editorial Credits:
Susan Evento, Managing Editor/Product Development; Elizabeth Jaffe, Senior Editor;
Sydney Wright and Charles Hunt, Designers; Kimberly Danger and Heidi Schoof,
Photo Researchers

Photo Credits:
Cover: Dwight Kuhn; Title Page: Dwight Kuhn (top left), Photo Network/Eric Berndt (bottom
left), Kirkendall/Spring (top right), Photo Network/Myrleen Ferguson Cate (bottom right);
Page 2: International Stock/Ryan Williams; Page 3: Jeff Greenberg/Photo Agora; Page 4:
Llewellyn/Pictor; Page 5: (clockwise from top left) Unicorn Stock Photos/Phyllis Kedl,
International Stock/John Michael, International Stock/Scott Barrow, Pictor; Page 6: Photo
Network; Page 7: Photo Network/Myrleen Ferguson Cate (left & right); Page 8: Diane Meyer,
Bob Daemmrich/Pictor (inset); Page 9: Pictor; Page 10: Kent & Donna Dannen; Page 11:
Kirkendall/Spring, Unicorn Stock Photos/Jeff Greenberg (inset); Page 12: John Elk III, Inga
Spence/TOM STACK & ASSOCIATES (inset); Page 13: Kent & Donna Dannen, Photo
Network/Eric Berndt (inset); Page 14: Jeff Strong/Photo Agora (left), Joanne Lotter/TOM
STACK & ASSOCIATES (inset); Page 15: James P. Rowan, International Stock/Mark Newman
(top inset), Kent & Donna Dannen (bottom inset); Page 16: Rob & Ann Simpson

1 2 3 4 5 6 06 05 04 03 02 01

People and Places

By Lauren Weidenman

Consulting Editor: Gail Saunders-Smith, Ph.D.
Consultants: Claudine Jellison and
Patricia Williams, Reading Recovery Teachers
Content Consultant: Andrew Gyory, Ph.D., American History

Yellow Umbrella Books

an imprint of Capstone Press
Mankato, Minnesota

People live in different kinds of places.

Some people live in places that have lots of people.

Some people live in places
that have few people.

Some people live in places
that are warm all year long.

And some people live in places
that have both warm
and cold weather.

Some people live in places
that are near oceans.
People swim in the ocean.

They play in the sand
and the waves.

Some people live
in places that are near
rivers, lakes, and ponds.

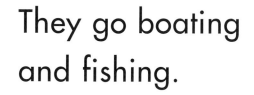

They go boating
and fishing.

People also skate on rivers, lakes, and ponds that freeze in the winter.

Some people live in places
that are hilly or near mountains.

People walk or hike in the hills
and mountains.

They also like to sled and ski.

Some people live in low lands between mountains. These low lands are called valleys.

People in valleys may live on farms and raise cows.

Some people live in wide, flat lands called plains.

People on plains may live on farms and grow plants like corn.

Some people live near places covered with trees, called forests.

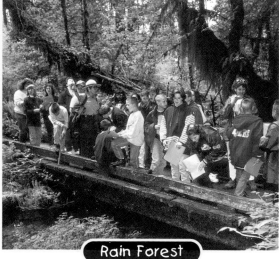
Temperate Forest

Rain Forest

Some people live near forests where a lot of rain falls. These are called rain forests. People can walk or hike in forests.

Some people live in places
where very little rain falls. These
dry places are called deserts.

People in the desert can study
the plants and animals
that live in these dry places.

People live in different kinds
of places.

In what kind of place do you live?

Words to Know/Index

Word Count: 254
Early-Intervention Levels: 13–16